I0606280

AMAZING TREES

Olivia Watson
Illustrated by Tjarda Borsboom

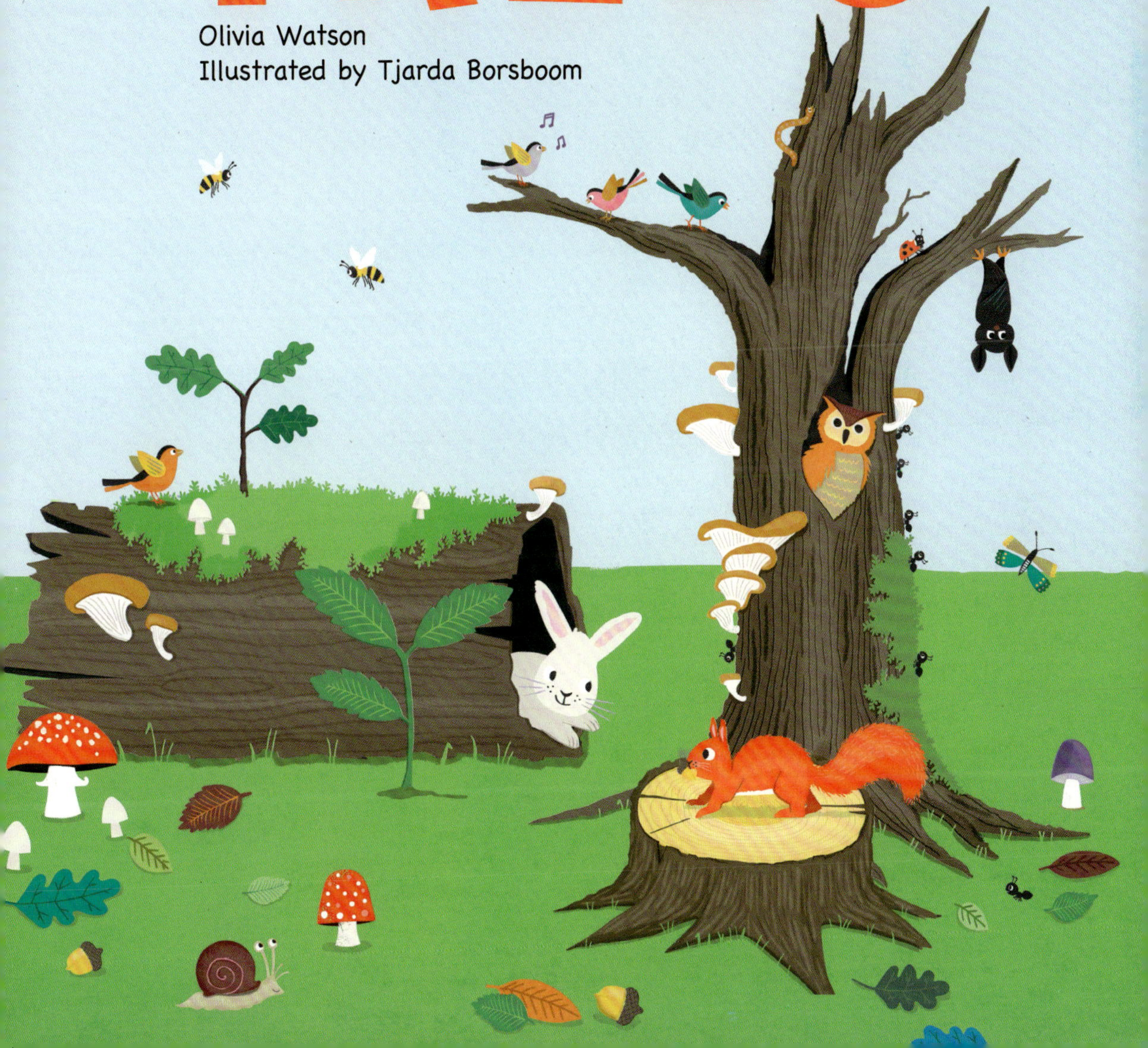

First published in 2024 by Hungry Tomato Ltd
F15, Old Bakery Studios, Blewetts Wharf, Malpas Road, Truro, Cornwall, TR1 1QH, UK.

A CIP catalog record for this book is available from the British Library.

ISBN 9781916598980

Printed in China

Discover more at
www.hungrytomato.com

Contents

What Is a Tree? 4
Family Trees 6
Nature's Compass 8
Tree Awards 10
Young or Old? 12
Stunning Looks 14
Smelliest Trees 16
Prize Trees 18
Did You Know? 20
Match Up the Pairs 22
Glossary 24

Words in **BOLD** can be found in the glossary.

Picture Credits

Abbreviations: m-middle, t-top, l-left, r-right, bg-background.

Shutterstock: Arnav Pratap Singh 19bl; elwynn 20tl; Georgios Tsichlis 18tl; Goinyk Production 23tl; Iakov Kalinin 23mr; IM_photo 21ml; Jeff Dalton 23tr; Kinggm.saleh 23bl; LizCoughlan 23br; Peter Turner Photography 18r; SEAN D THOMAS 21tr; Shootz photography 23ml; Rafael Novais 19tr.

Every effort has been made to trace the copyright holders, and we apologize in advance for any unintentional omissions. We would be pleased to insert the appropriate acknowledgments in any subsequent edition of this publication.

What Is a Tree?

Trees are living things that can be found almost everywhere on Earth! They are important for people and nature. Trees come in all shapes and sizes, but most have the same four parts.

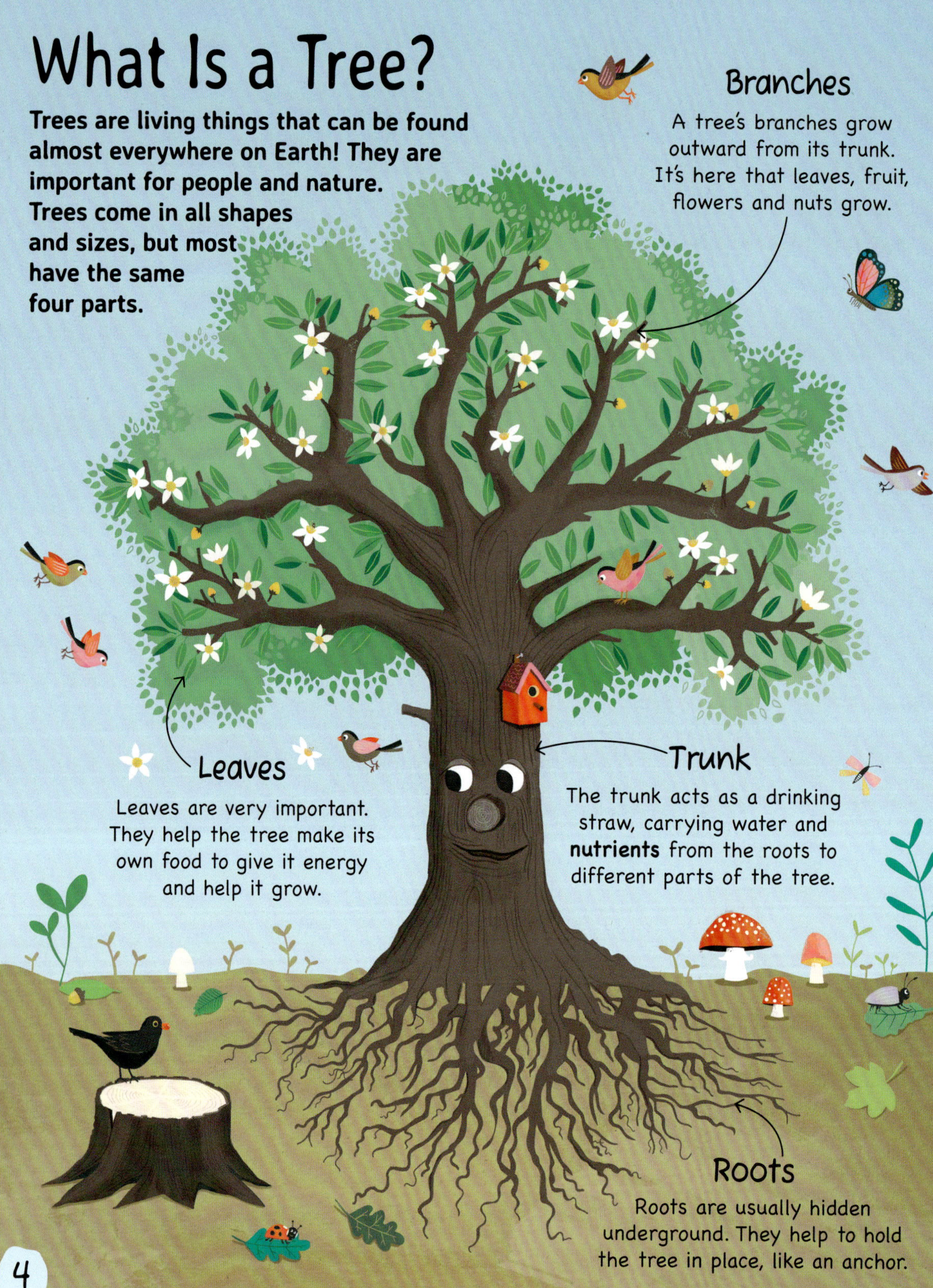

Apple seed

Twig

Fruit

Some trees have other features, such as fruit, which are full of hidden seeds. Some are tiny, like apple seeds, and some are much bigger, like avocado seeds.

Avocado seed

Not a tree

Some plants that we call trees aren't trees at all! Cacti and boojum aren't made of wood, and palms don't have branches, so they don't count!

Cactus

Boojum tree

Palm tree

Family Trees

Trees often work together to help each other survive. Sometimes they even work with other living things!

Friendly fungi?

Some mushrooms hurt trees by making them sick! Others help them by sharing nutrients back and forth.

Wood wide web

Scientists think that **fungi** help trees talk to each other by joining their roots together. They call this the "wood wide web"!

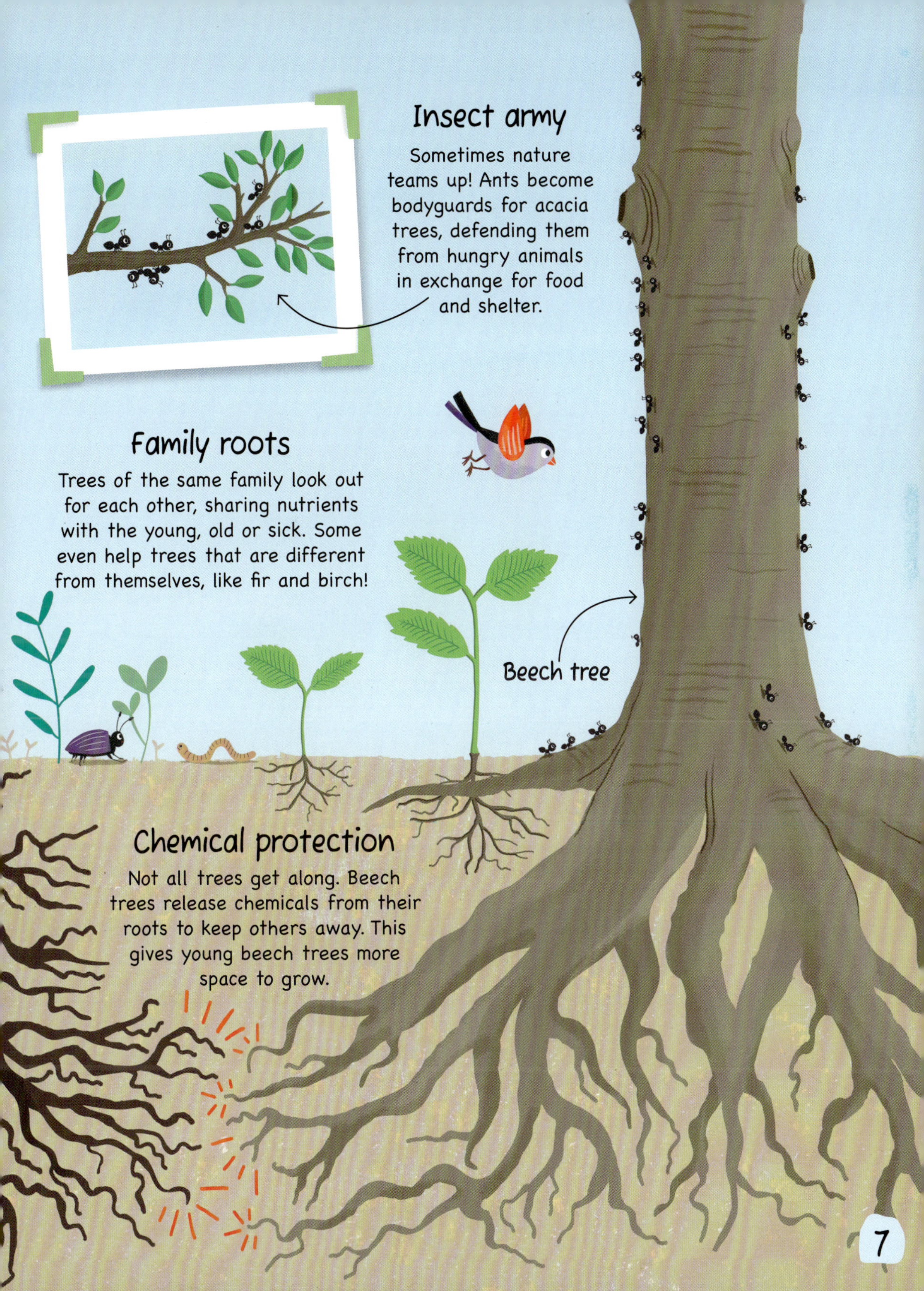
Insect army
Sometimes nature teams up! Ants become bodyguards for acacia trees, defending them from hungry animals in exchange for food and shelter.
Family roots
Trees of the same family look out for each other, sharing nutrients with the young, old or sick. Some even help trees that are different from themselves, like fir and birch!
Beech tree
Chemical protection
Not all trees get along. Beech trees release chemicals from their roots to keep others away. This gives young beech trees more space to grow.

Nature's Compass

The way trees grow can be affected by the weather! The direction of the wind and sunshine can make a big difference to how they look.

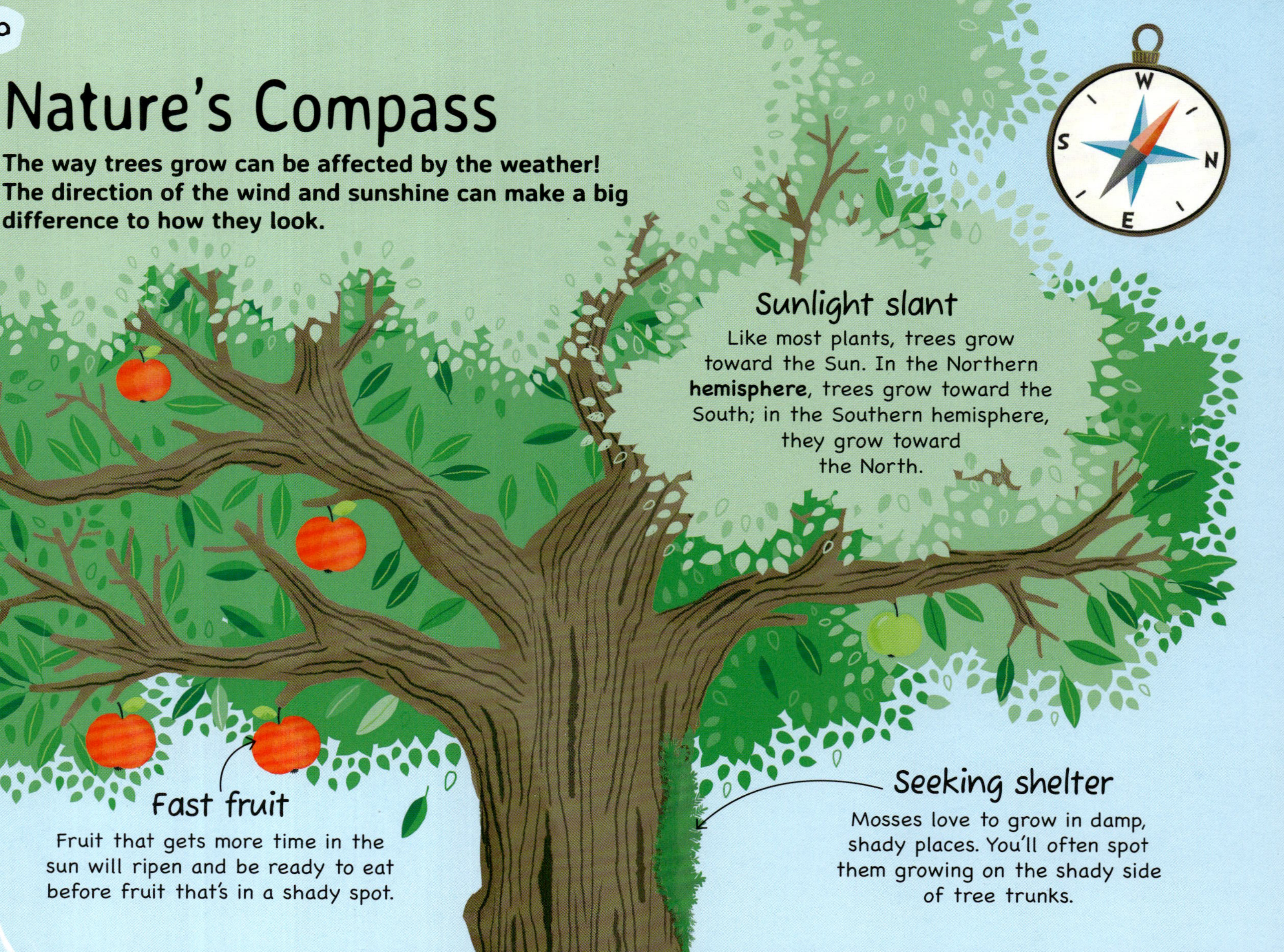

Sunlight slant

Like most plants, trees grow toward the Sun. In the Northern **hemisphere**, trees grow toward the South; in the Southern hemisphere, they grow toward the North.

Fast fruit

Fruit that gets more time in the sun will ripen and be ready to eat before fruit that's in a shady spot.

Seeking shelter

Mosses love to grow in damp, shady places. You'll often spot them growing on the shady side of tree trunks.

Prevailing wind

In most places, the wind blows from one direction more than others. This is called a "prevailing wind", and it affects how trees grow.

Wild winds

Trees hit by wind don't grow as big, leaving rows of trees growing to different heights! This shape is called the "wedge effect".

Super strength

To cope with strong winds, some trees thicken parts of their trunk and roots to stop themselves being blown down.

Happy heart

They don't beat like ours, but trees have hearts too! Heartwood is extra strong, dark wood that's hidden inside the trunk.

Tree Awards

These record-breaking trees are some of the most impressive!

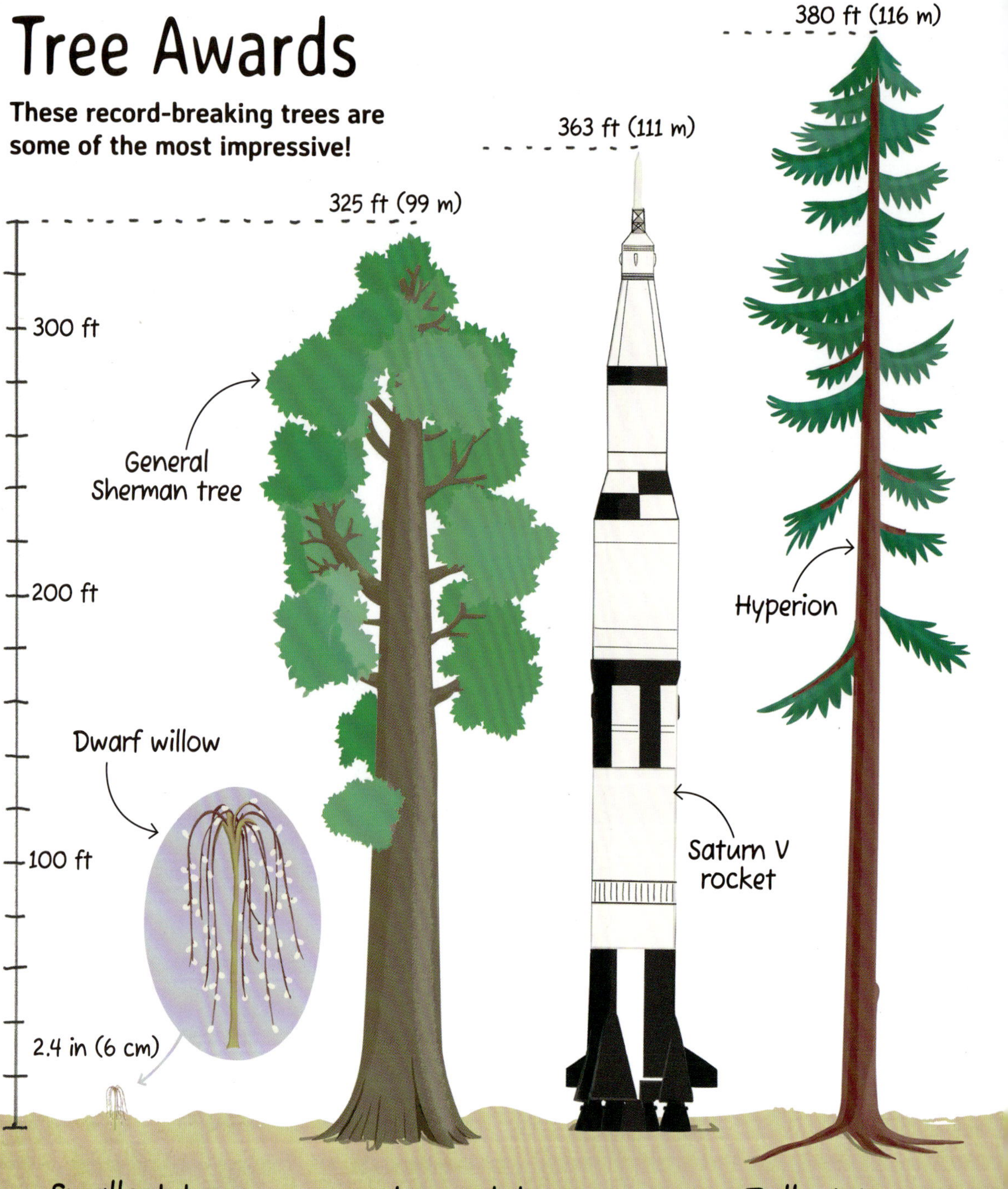

380 ft (116 m)

363 ft (111 m)

325 ft (99 m)

300 ft

200 ft

100 ft

2.4 in (6 cm)

General Sherman tree

Hyperion

Dwarf willow

Saturn V rocket

Smallest tree

The dwarf willow is the smallest tree, growing to only 2.4 inches (6 cm) tall!

Largest tree

The General Sherman in California, USA, is the largest tree in the world!

Tallest tree

The Hyperion redwood tree is even taller than one of the tallest rockets: Saturn V.

Widest tree

At a whopping 46 feet (14 m), El Árbol del Tule in Mexico is the widest tree in the world!

Oldest tree

The Great Basin bristlecone pine, called Methuselah, that's growing in the USA is almost 5,000 years old!

Young or Old?

Trees are some of the oldest living things on our planet. They can't live forever, but even at the end of their lives, they're interesting plants!

Bell bottom

Old trees stop growing up, but keep growing outward, giving them bell-shaped trunks. Dying trees that stay standing are called snags.

Nutrient delivery

Dead trees release nutrients into the soil, making it better for new plants and trees to grow.

Life after death

Even dead trees keep forests alive! Hollow logs make great animal homes, and rotting wood is yummy food for some fungi.

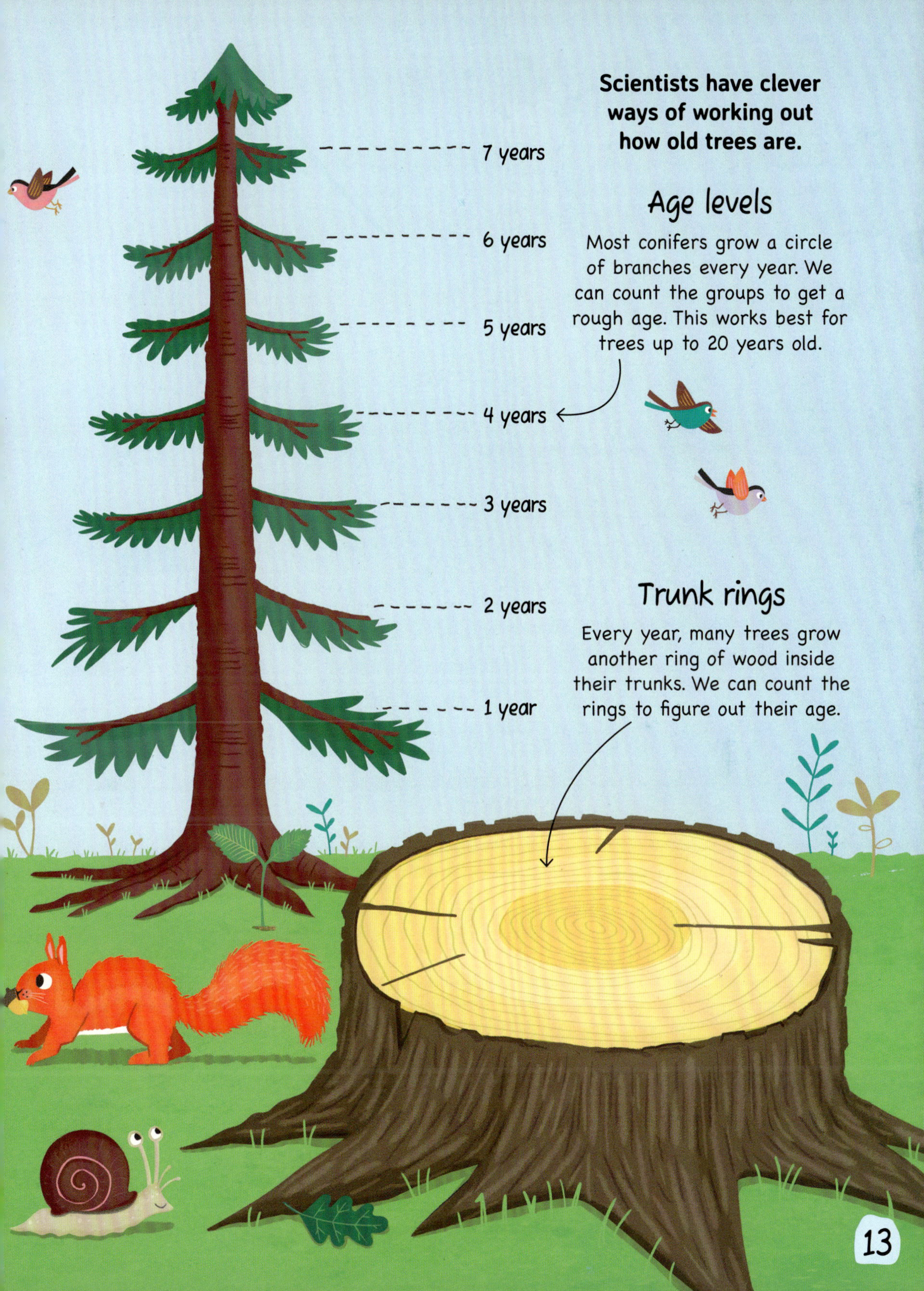

Scientists have clever ways of working out how old trees are.

Age levels

Most conifers grow a circle of branches every year. We can count the groups to get a rough age. This works best for trees up to 20 years old.

Trunk rings

Every year, many trees grow another ring of wood inside their trunks. We can count the rings to figure out their age.

Stunning Looks

There are so many amazing-looking trees around the world. Which one do you think stands out the most?

Crooked Forest

These curved trees in Poland are surrounded by straight trees! No one knows why some are this strange shape.

Bonsai tree

These tiny trees can be trained to grow into beautiful shapes. The art of shaping bonsai is more than 1,000 years old.

Dragon blood tree

This spooky tree is named for its thick red **sap**, which people once believed was the blood of dragons!

Silk cotton tree temples

Giant silk cotton trees have taken over an abandoned temple in Cambodia, twisting their roots around the stones.

Prison tree

This **sacred** boab tree in Australia, with its wide, hollow trunk, is claimed to have once been used to hold prisoners!

Topiary trees

From twirls to animal shapes, topiary is the art of creating and shaping living masterpieces out of trees!

Cannonball tree

Look out! This tree has big, heavy cannonball-like fruits that fall to the ground when ripe.

Smelliest Trees

Some plants smell good enough to eat, while others might put you off your food!

Banana shrub

These pretty yellow flowers smell just like bananas!

Caramel tree

These leaves smell like caramel and toffee.

Some trees' smells come from their flowers, and some come from their leaves!

Yellowtail

These bright clusters of flowers smell like pineapple. Yum yum!

Callery pear

Don't get tricked by these pretty **blossoms** – they smell like rotting fish. Ew!

Ginkgo

This tree stinks! Most people think it smells like dirty gym socks or dog poop.

Kapok

This tree's flowers may smell horrible to us, but bats love them!

White spruce

When broken, these needles smell like a stinky skunk!

Prize Trees

Our big wide world is home to many extraordinary plants with fascinating features and clever characteristics. There are so many to celebrate, including these prize plants that really stand out from the crowd.

Thousands of tourists visit this tree every year.

The trunk is completely hollow!

Ancient and amazing

The Olive Tree of Vouves in Greece is thought to be one of the oldest olive trees in the world! Gnarled and twisting, this tree still produces olives, despite being ancient. Scientists don't know exactly how old it is but they think it's at least 2,000 years old!

Living fossil

One of the most extraordinary trees is the Wollemi pine. One of the world's rarest plants, dating back to the time of the dinosaurs, this **coniferous** tree was considered **extinct** for millions of years until a small group was found in Australia in 1994.

Needle-like leaves which darken with age.

This **species** is **native** to Australia.

Very few of these trees still grow in the world.

Far and wide

Pando, also known as the "trembling tree" is a **colony** of quaking aspen trees in Utah, USA. Although it's made up of more than 40,000 trees, they all grew from one seed and are connected by their roots, which makes the colony one single living organism!

Pando may be thousands of years old!

Each single tree lives between 100 and 130 years.

It covers 106 acres!

This tree is constantly growing to cover a bigger space.

Fascinating forest

Located in India, the Great Banyan tree is one of the most unusual trees ever, and the largest of its kind. Rather than growing underground, its roots grow outward and downward from its branches, creating a complex web of wood that looks like a tangle of trunks!

It's **pollinated** by a single species of wasp.

Did You Know?

Trees are pretty amazing! Every living creature needs trees to survive; the world wouldn't be the way it is today if we didn't have them. Did you know these amazing facts about trees?

Jaboticaba berries grow on the

TRUNK AND BRANCHES

of the tree, rather than among the leaves!

Trees have been on Earth for more than

350 MILLION YEARS!

That's way before dinosaurs walked the Earth!

The Manchineel tree is considered the most **POISONOUS** tree in the world!

As the **bark** peels off the rainbow eucalyptus tree, the trunk becomes **MULTI-COLORED!**

Giant sequoias have the **THICKEST BARK** of any tree. It can be thicker than 40 inches (1 m)!

Some people call the oak tree **"THE KING OF THE FOREST"** because it's so strong and lives for so long.

Match Up the Pairs

Can you match up the fact boxes (below) with the correct tree (right)? Flip back through the book if you need a hint!

1.

I am the smallest tree in the world.

2.

I'm the world's oldest living tree. I'm almost 5,000 years old!

3.

My blossoms may be pretty, but they smell like rotting fish!

4.

Humans used to think my red sap was the blood of dragons!

5.

I'm the widest tree in the world!

6.

I grow big, heavy fruit that falls to the ground when ripe.

Dwarf willow tree

El Árbol del Tule tree

Great Basin bristlecone tree

Callery pear tree

Cannonball tree

Dragon blood tree

Have you matched them all?

Answers can be found on page 24.

Glossary

Bark - the tough outer layer of a woody plant stem or root, such as a tree trunk.

Blossoms - the flowers of stone fruit trees like plums, cherries and apples.

Colony - a large group of living things that live together and came from a single ancestor.

Coniferous - trees that have narrow, hard leaves called needles or scales.

Extinct - when a species no longer exists.

Fungi - (the plural of fungus). A group of living things, including mushrooms, molds, and yeasts, that are neither plants nor animals.

Hemisphere - half of the Earth, divided by an invisible line through the middle. The countries in the top half are Northern and the ones in the bottom half are Southern.

Native - something that naturally grows or lives in a particular area.

Nutrients - substances or ingredients that plants and animals need to live and grow.

Poisonous - something that is very harmful and can cause severe illness or death.

Pollinated - (verb) the process of pollen (see below) being moved from one flower to another - often by an insect - so the plant can make new seeds.

Pollen - a dusty powder made by some plants. It is used to produce new seeds.

Sacred - something that is spiritual, and/or worthy of awe and respect.

Sap - a watery substance that comes out of a plant or tree.

Species - a group of living things that are the same as each other. For example, African forest elephants and African bush elephants are two different species.

Answers to Match Up the Pairs

Answers: 1. Dwarf willow tree, 2. Great Basin bristlecone tree, 3. Callery pear tree, 4. Dragon blood tree, 5. El Árbol del Tule tree, 6. Cannonball tree.